Mosaics by Anthony Vandyk

DOROTHY L. HILDE

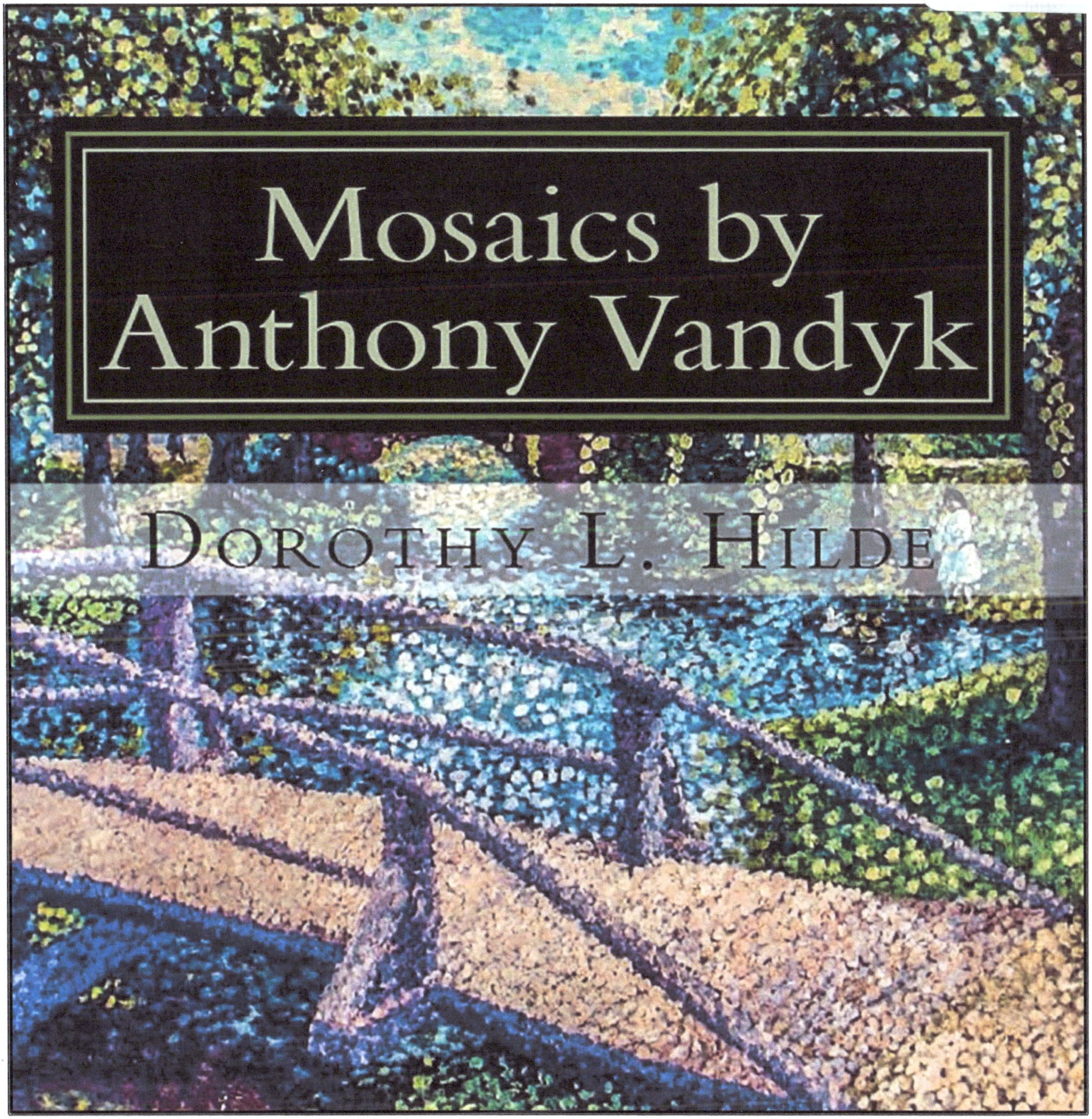

Printed in the United States of America, Columbia, SC.

ISBN-13: 978-1545377093
ISBN-10: 154537709X

First Printing, 2018
Language: English

Publisher: CreateSpace Independent Publishing Platform; 1 edition (February 2018)
www.createspace.com

Collection of Mosaic Oil paintings of Anthony (Hank) Vandyk.

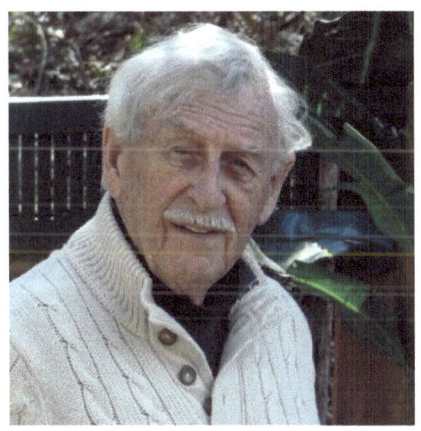

Hank, a Canadian-Dutch artist with an international reputation, creates works of art that are comparable to that of Claude Monet. His mosaic series has been showcased in various mainstream galleries around the world.

Mosaic – *a collection of tiny pieces of glass, pebbles, stone, or other objects arranged artistically to create a design. Hank's mosaic series is a play of ovals and circles, which were produced by applying thousands of tiny dabs of paint with a palette knife.*

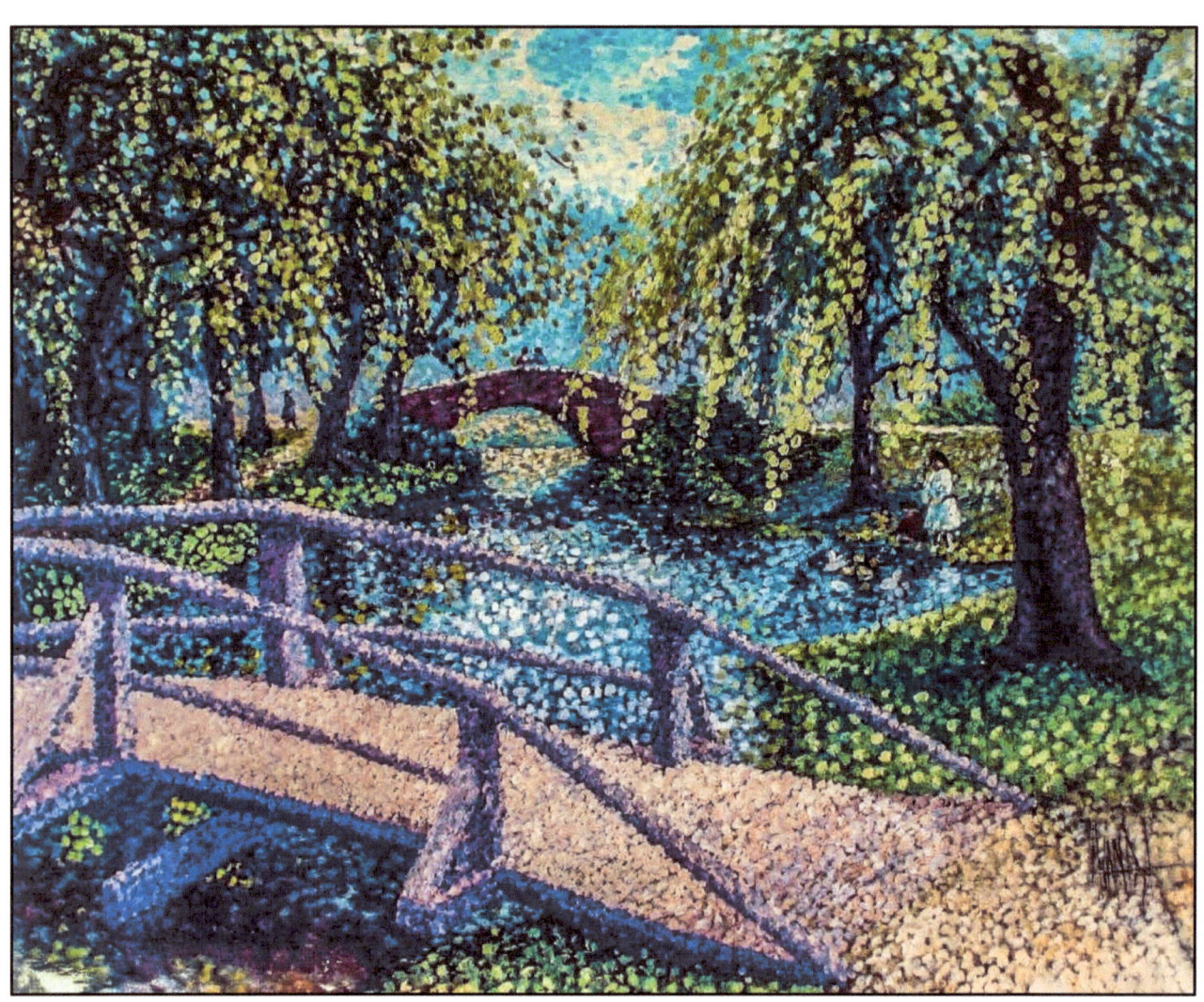

The Girl in Stanley Park

This piece is similar to Monet's Water Lilies and Japanese bridge, 1897–99. It is a representation of a spring day at the famous Stanley Park, Vancouver, BC, Canada.

The Mother and Foal

"Mother and Foal" is Hank's favourite creation. Remarkably, this piece took over 360 hours to paint and has such a maternal feel. As depicted, the mare reached its neck downwards in a stirring curve to caress its foal, while the foal's neck curves upwards to suckle. This creatively represents the complete circle of a Mother's love for her young.

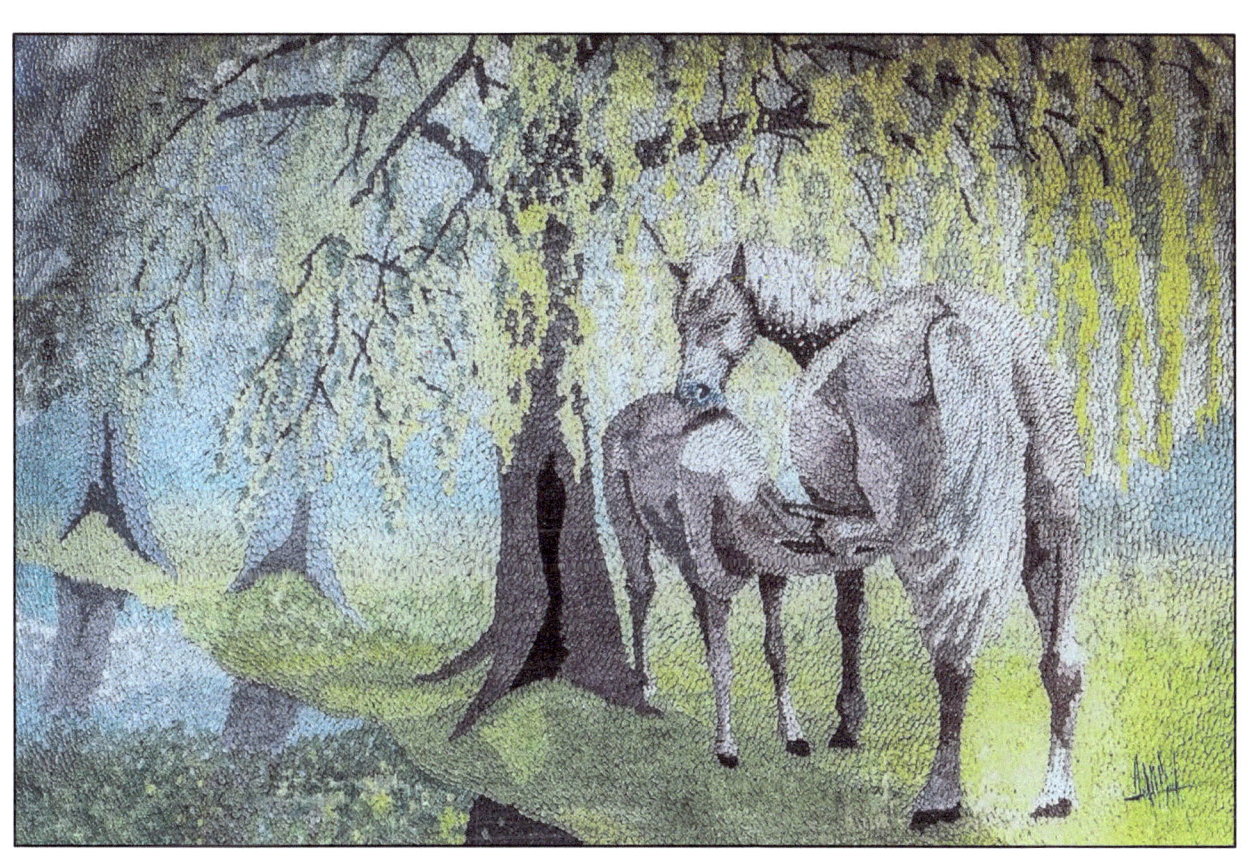

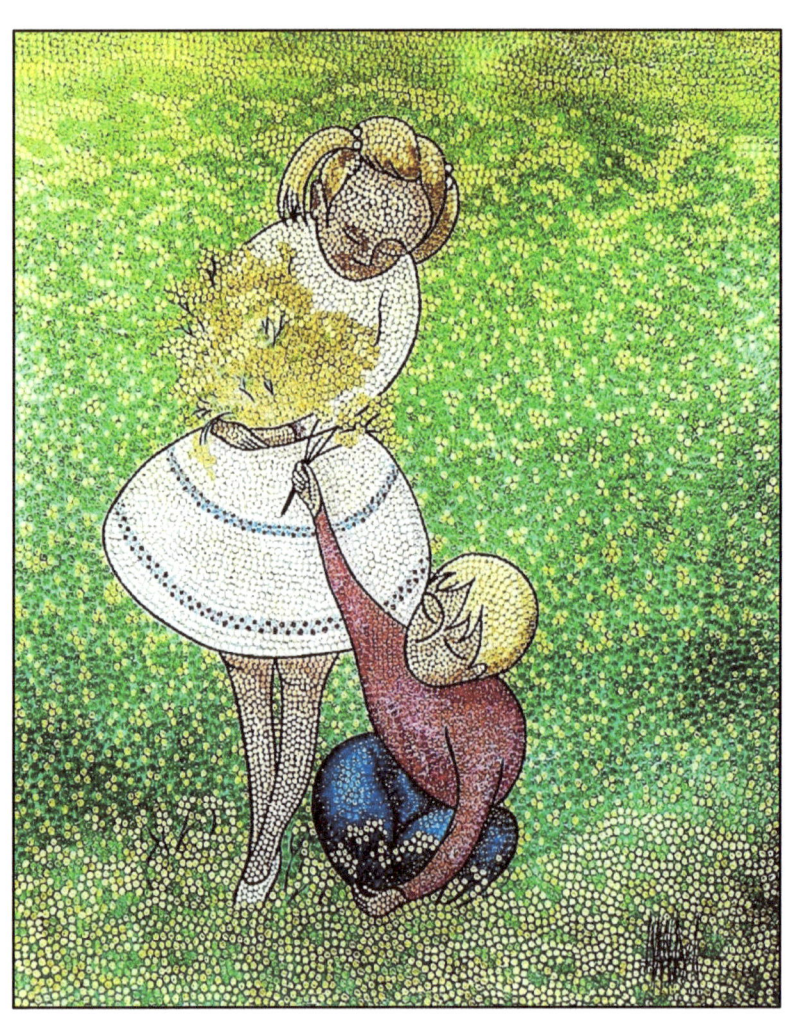

Picking Daisies

The Netherlands has been at the centre of the world's flower trade since the 1950s. Interestingly, the Dutch's national flower, tulips, is not the only flower that decorates its countryside as most people seem to believe. Daisies, too, are a cultivated variety of flower in the Netherlands. The name "daisy" is derived from the Old English word "daes eag," meaning "day's eye" — stemmed from the way its beautiful petals bloom (open) at dawn. Daisies are, in many cultures, a representation of purity and innocence. Markedly, a daisy is actually two flowers in one.

The piece, Picking Daisies, portrays the courtship of a young man and his sweetheart: their hearts, akin to that of a daisy — two flowers in one.

Bathers in Stream

On a hot summer day, two young ladies were wading in a stream when one of them stubbed her toe against a rock submerged in the stream's bed. In this piece Hank portrays her discomfort and a friend's empathy: She grimaced in obvious pain, bent her back, bowed her head, and upturned her foot to get a view of her bloodied toe. Her friend placed her hand on her shoulder in a show of compassion.

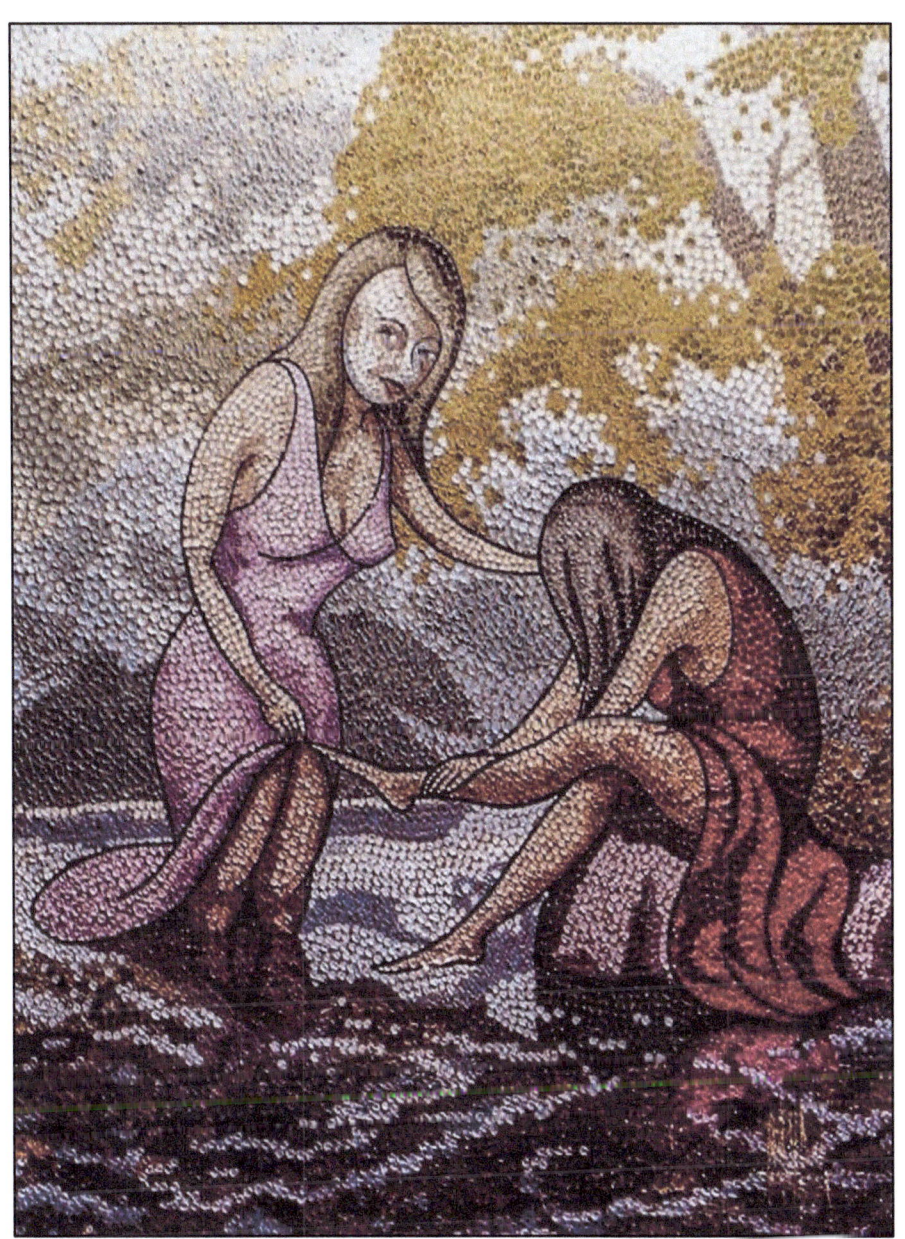

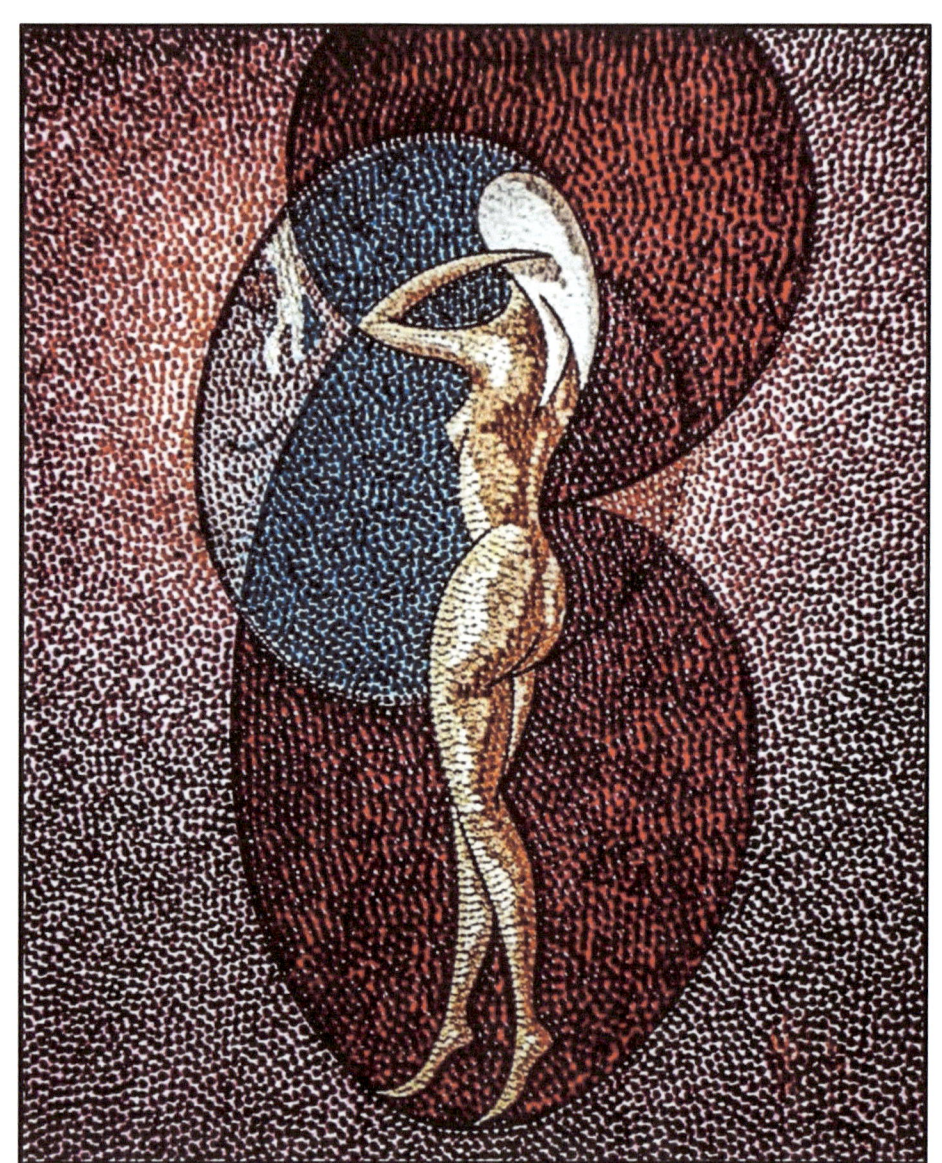

The Blue Mirror

What is a reflection? A reflection can represent a true image of oneself. A redirection of light that struck the surface of one's body; a light that is not absorbed by the body. Additionally, a reflection can stand as a person's emotion at that point in time. The Blue Mirror creation captures both the physical image and emotional state of an individual. The woman depicted in this piece is unhappy with her reflection. The blue colour inside the middle circle denotes her state of melancholy, while the red circles represent the stark contrast to her actual physical image. The entire piece completes a visual reflection of the bold and empowering strength of today's woman.

Easter Sunday Parade

The Easter Sunday Parade is a longstanding American tradition, which began, in the 1870s, as a spontaneous event in New York. Female participants traditionally don a fashionable attire, a hat, and a pair of gloves; while the male participants wear a suit and tie. Notably, the New York's Easter Parade was one of the main cultural events in the United States from the 1880s-1950s. At the event, individuals would strive to impress other participants and onlookers with their distinct finery.

In this piece, Hank depicts three ladies, their tight-knit circle with a tree branch curved above their heads. Also illustrated is the sweeping motion of the path that lays beneath their feet. The bunnies in the women's hats are a playful indication of the fun family and friends have during the yearly event.

Vancouver's Stanley park holds this event every year with an Easter egg hunt for the children, a train ride through the park, mini golf, face painting, and the meeting of the Easter Bunny.

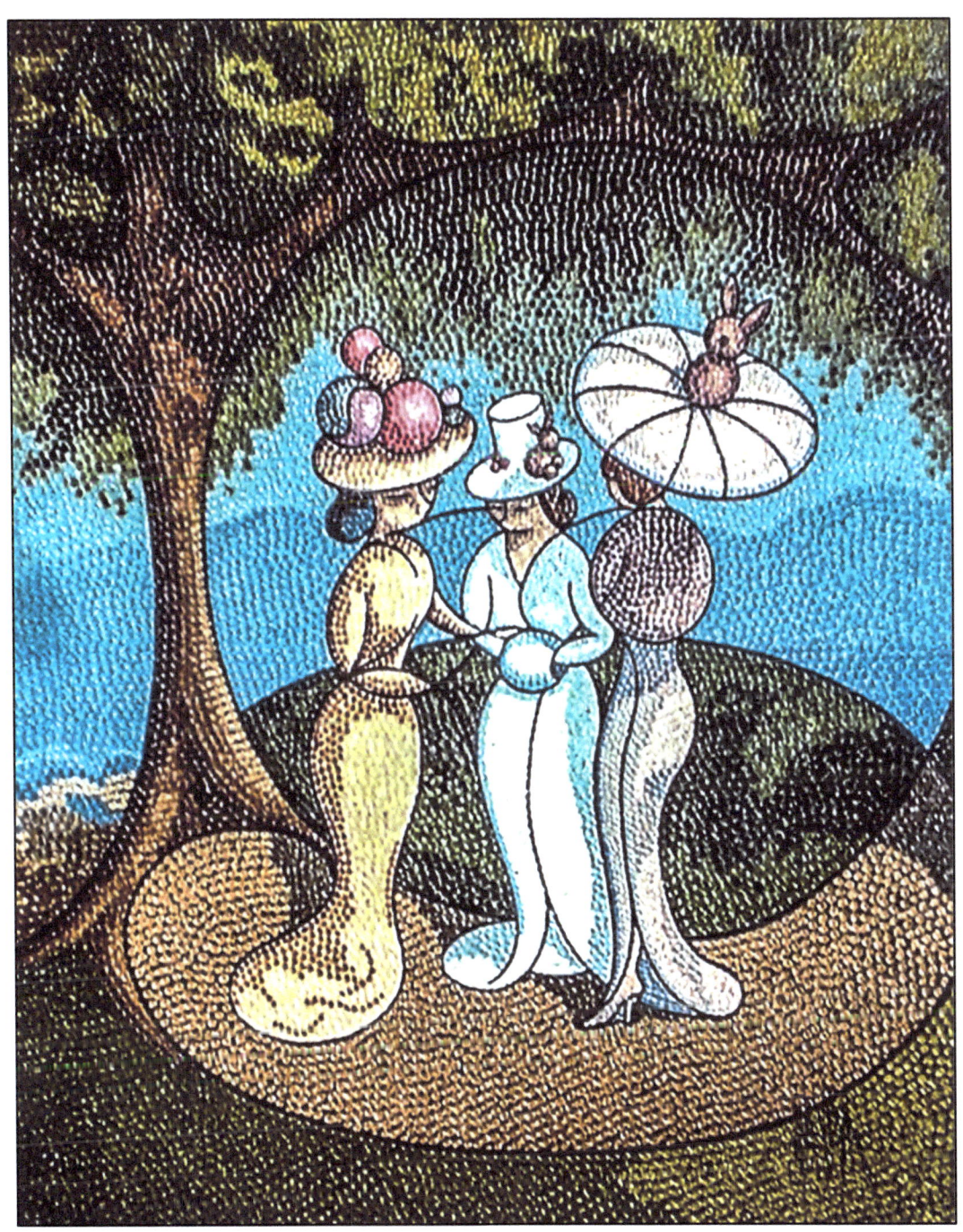

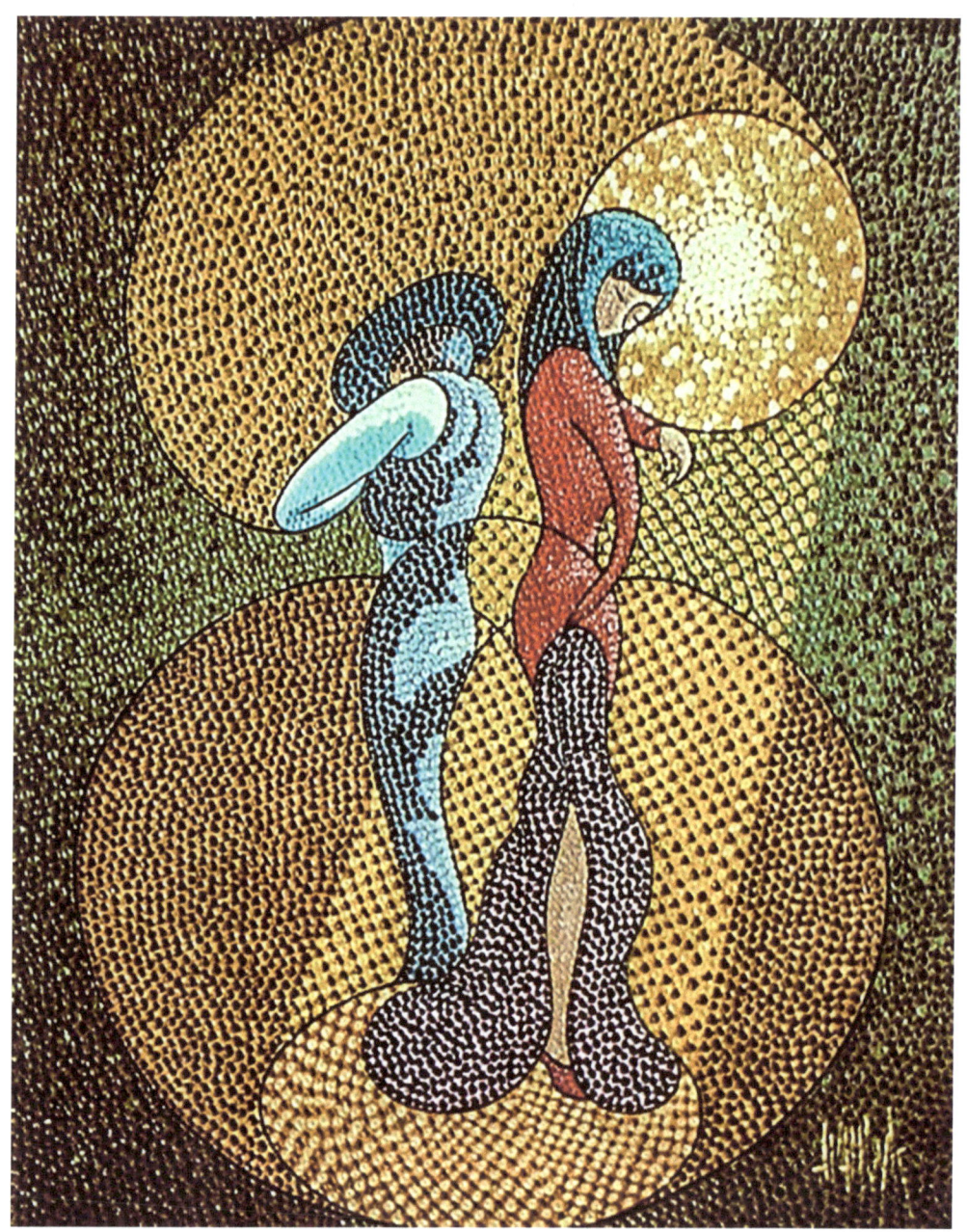

The Flamenco Dancers

Flamenco is an intimate kind of music with its origin wrapped in a bit of a mystery. In some corners, Flamenco is said to have originated in Andalusia in the VIII to the XV centuries when Spain was under Arabian rule. The music and musical instruments were modified and adopted by Christians, Jews, and, eventually, gypsies. Flamenco is not only about the music, but also a tradition. Flamenco clubs are decorated with eye-catching mosaic tiles, ornately wrought ironwork, and a sense of liveliness—a vitality of life itself.

Hank has encased the feel of the atmosphere, a guitarist, and a dancer moving to the rhythmic beat. This piece portrays a juerga (Flamenco party) with a small group of friends, at midnight somewhere in the South of Spain.

Mother and Child I

In this piece, Hank depicts a mother's benevolence and warmth toward her child. Her loving arms provide a form of sanctuary from the wiles of the world. Hank once again uses ellipses to interpret this bond. The meniscus to the right pulls the child into the mother's chest; the crescent to the left, reassurance with her caress. The mother's cheek against the child's head creates a unique figure-of-eight reinforcing a mother's benevolence and warmth toward her child.

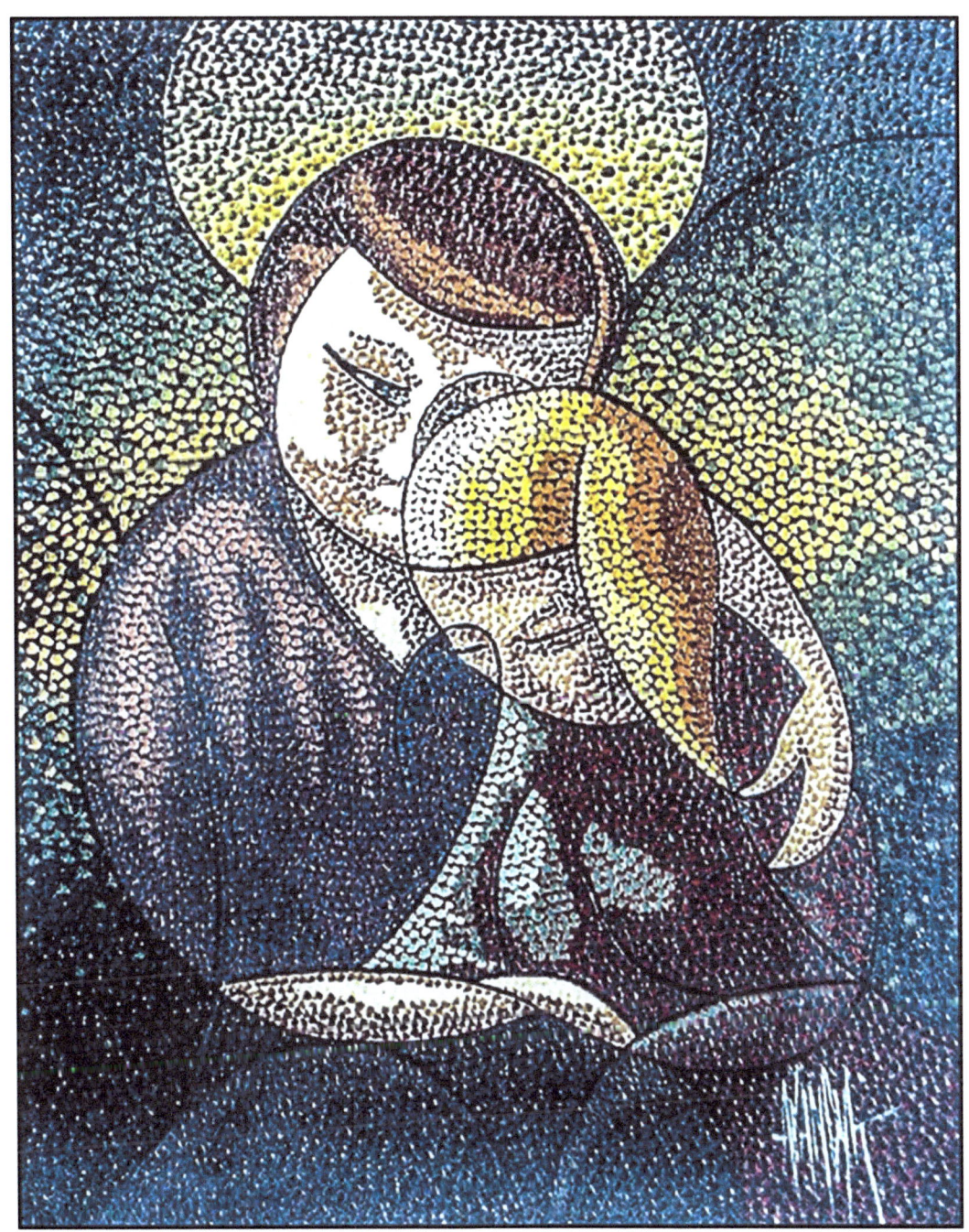

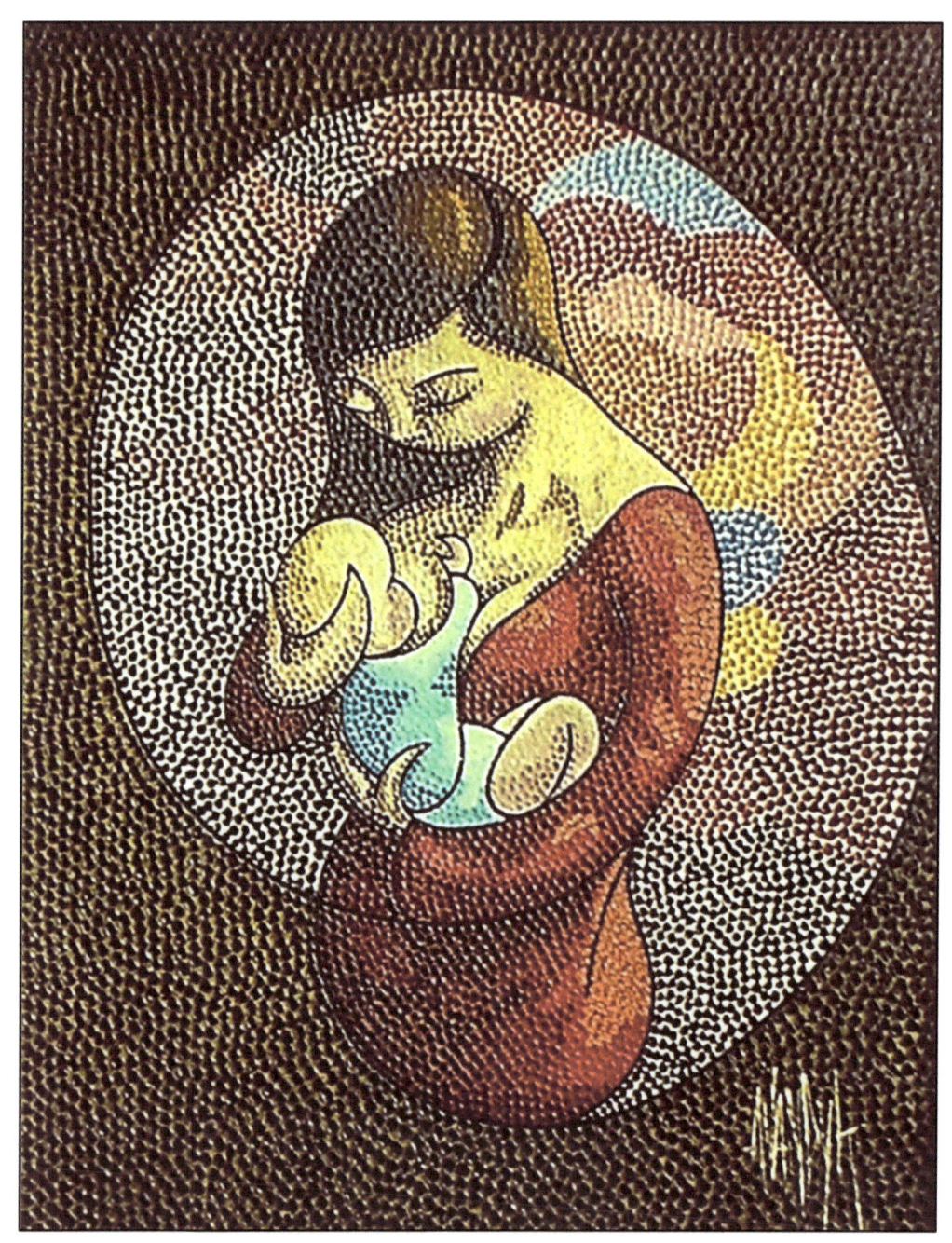

Mother and Child II

No bond is more intimate than that which exists between a mother and her child.

In this very heartwarming piece, Hank's depicts a mother breastfeeding her infant. The mother's arms took the shape of a half-moon, while the roundness of the child's back is a reflection of the unconditional love and support from a mother to her child. The mother's hand cradling the baby's head portrays a sense of trust, while the mother's gaze envelops the warmth, peace, and serenity of a child.

Mother and Child III

Another work of art in Hank's mother-child collection, exhibiting a mother's love. This piece illustrates a mother lovingly gazing down at her infant son who is in her hands. She is seen cradling him, which seems to form an "S" curve, representing the support provided by a mother's love.

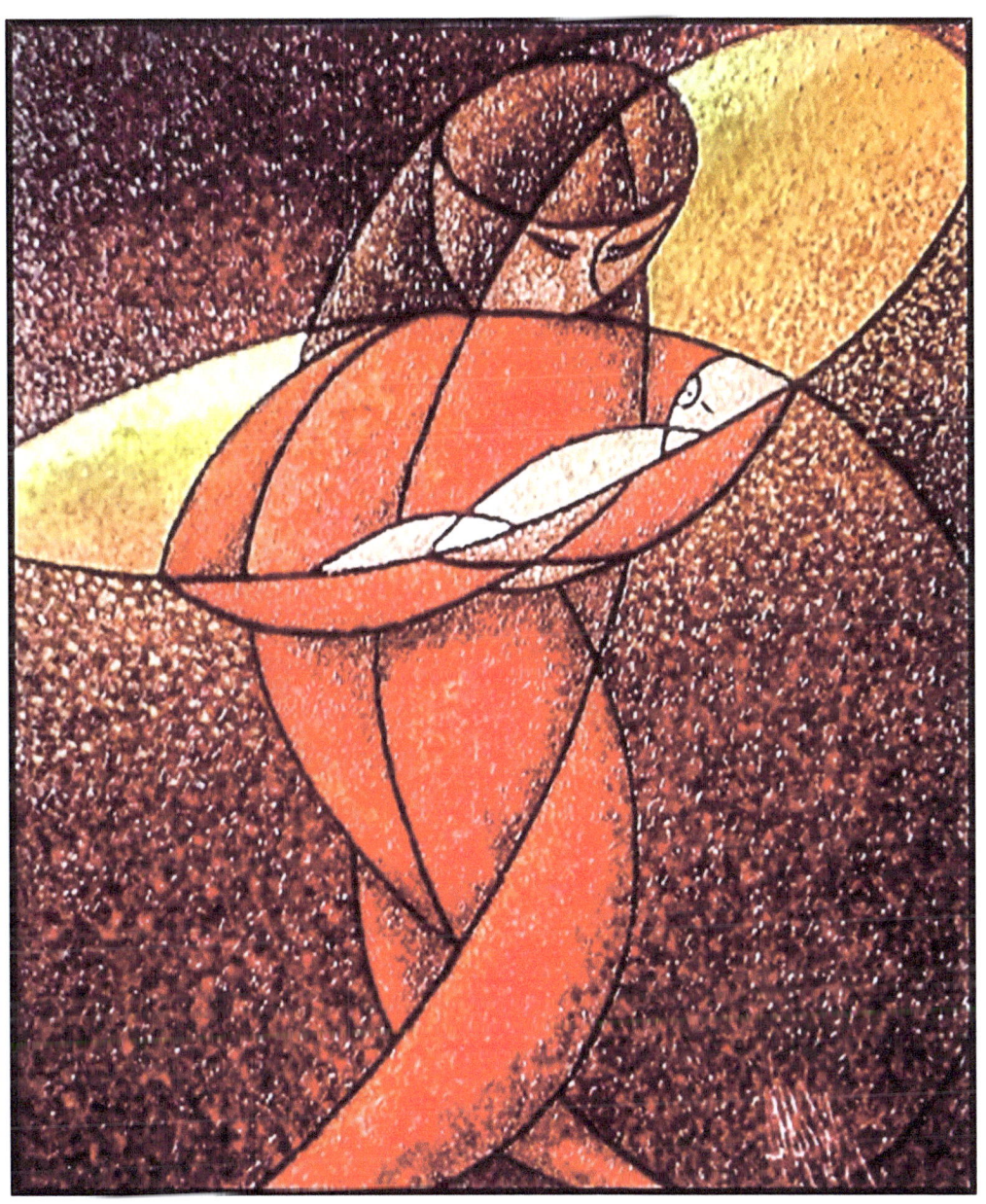

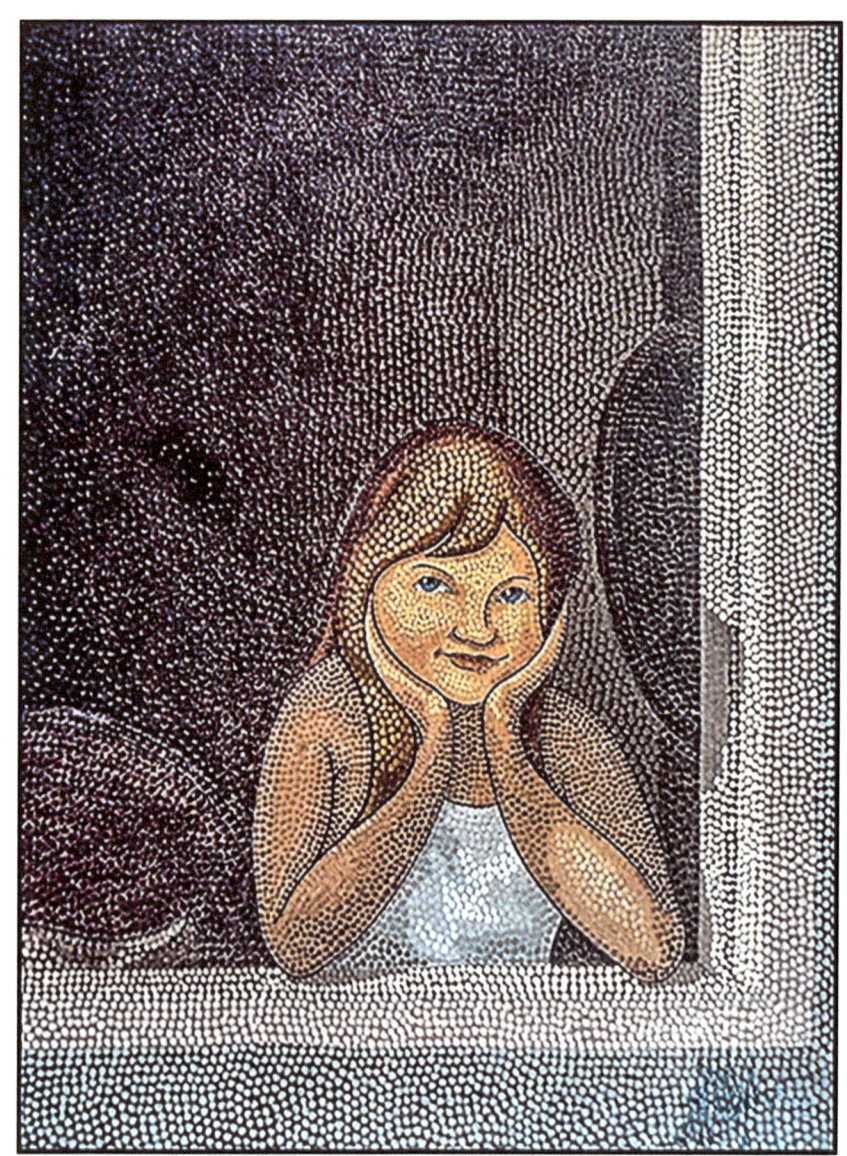

The Girl in The Window

This piece depicts a young girl daydreaming by her open window. What could she be fantasizing about: a faraway land, a part in a play, a new love? Her arms are positioned in a perfect "V" shape as if they were the trunks of a tree supporting her fantasies.

Bringing in the crops

A sickle is a hand-held tool used for harvesting grain with a blade so sharp that the wielder can either draw it inward or swing it outward against the base of the crop.

In this piece, Hank's choice of warm goldened tones: a mixture of reds; oranges, browns, and yellows make a bold contrast of colors. The arcs of the sickle and the man's back complement each other supporting the man's determination and strength, as he wields the curved sickle and harvests the wheat.

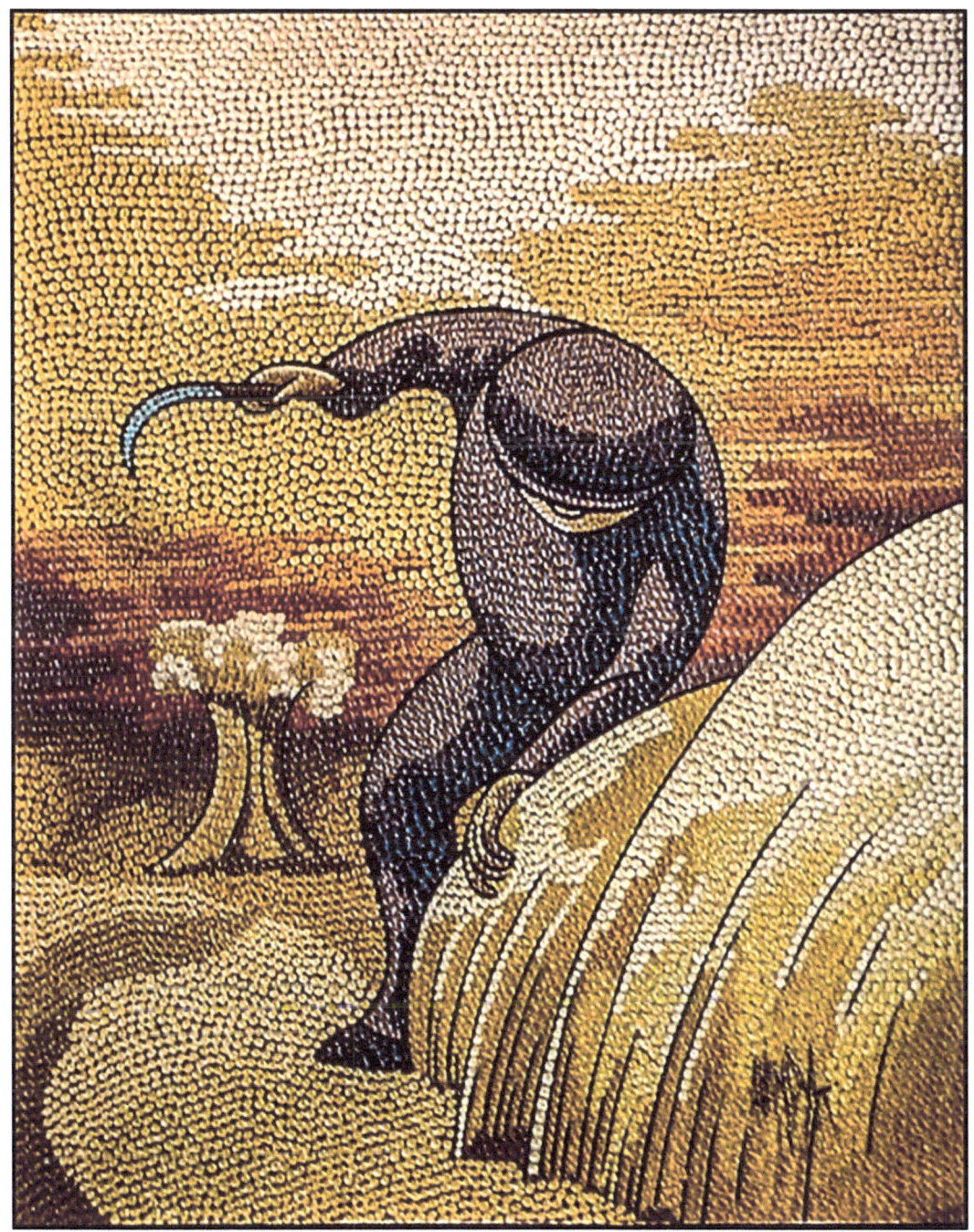

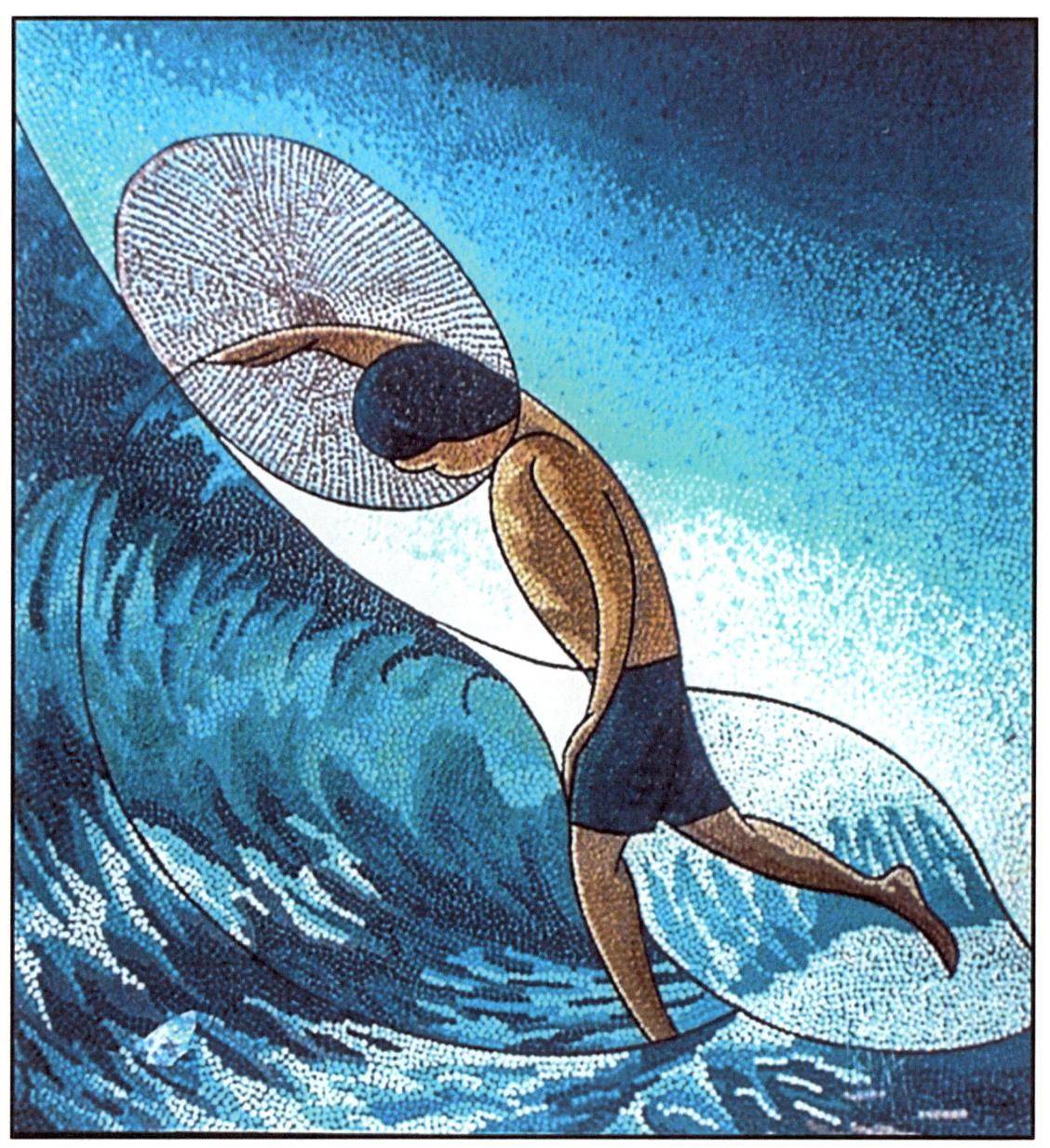

Mexican Fisher Boy

In this piece, Hank employed several geometrical designs: figure-of-eights, spheres, arcs, and points of intersection which all meld together intimating a young boy fishing by hand in the ocean in Queretaro, Mexico.

Three Men in a Boat

The Three Men in a Boat piece was inspired by men fishing in a small boat in Spain surrounded by squawking gulls anxiously awaiting their share. While the deep rich burgundies, purples, and blues evoke a strong moody feeling—a sense of impending doom.

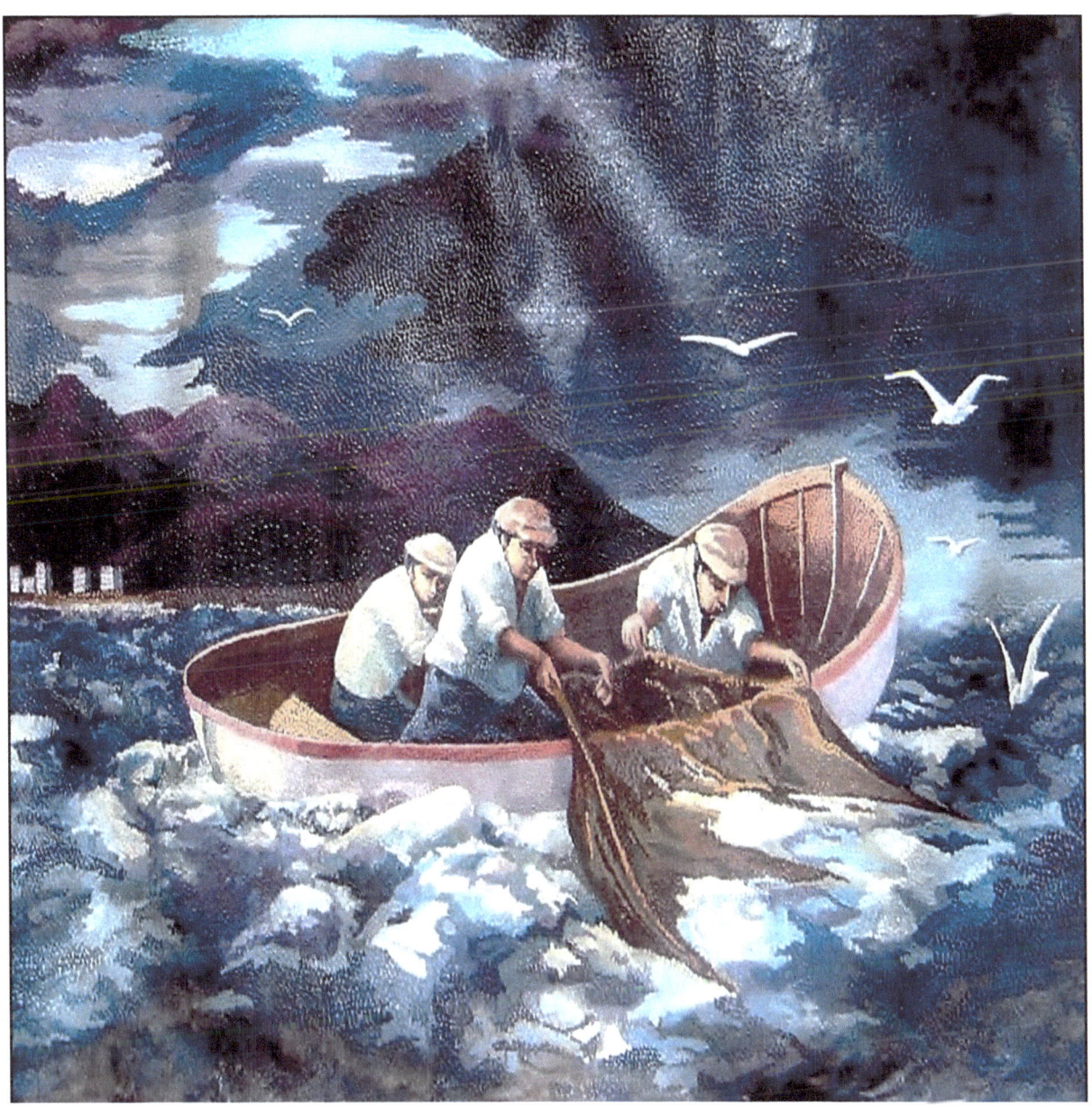

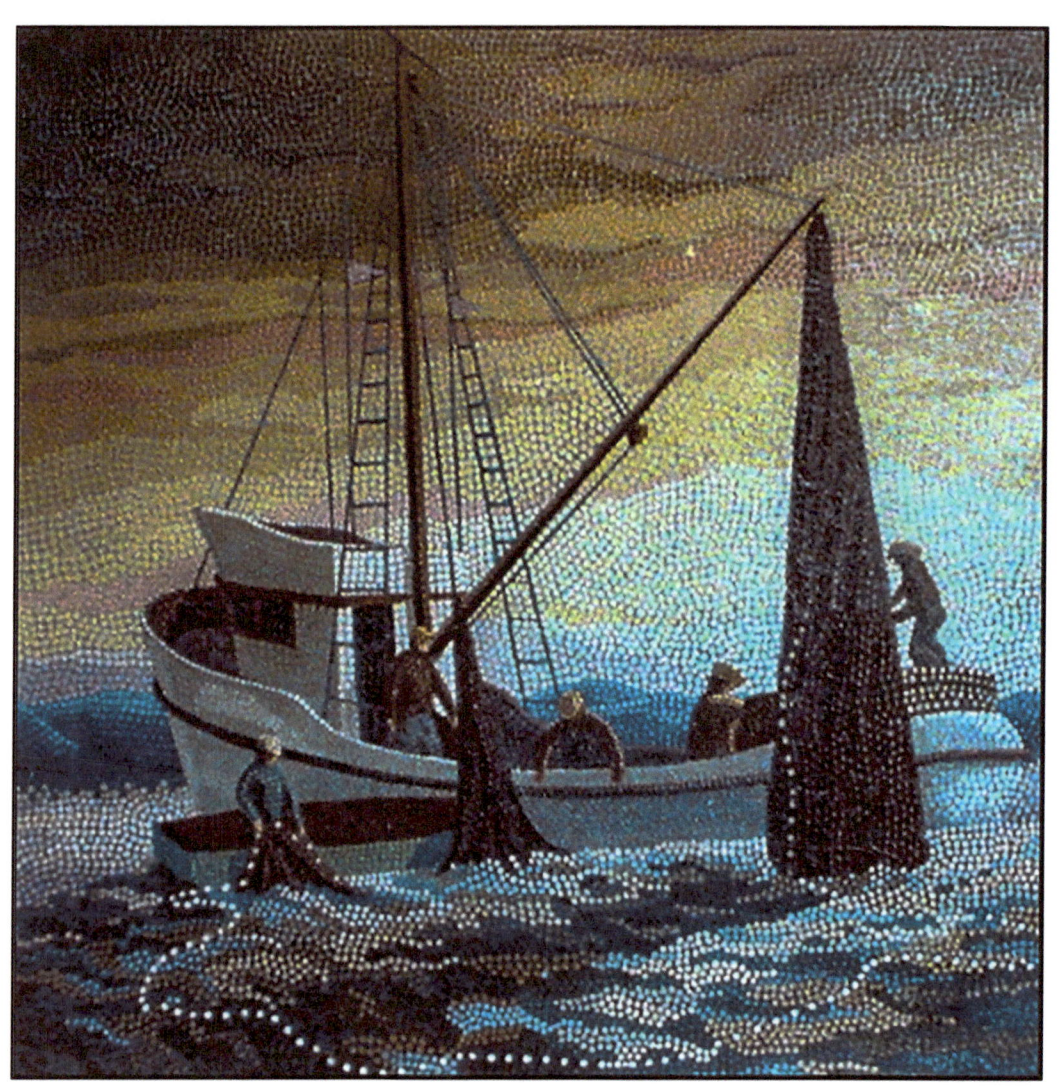

Tugboat Fisherman

In this piece, Hank depicts the Boat BCP45. BCP45 is a trawler that spent most of her life catching salmon. The image of the BCP45 graced the back of the Canadian $5.00 bill from 1972 to 1986. In 1986, the BCP45 was featured in the opening parade of Expo '86 in Vancouver, BC. Subsequently, after 68 years of service as a salmon seiner, gillnetter, beam trawler, and tow-off for the winter herring, the BCP45 was retired in 1996. She now resides at the Campbell River Maritime Heritage Centre.

The Blood of a Whale

This mosaic was first painted with a coat of red paint, depicting the bloodshed from the killing of whales in the sea, which incarnadines the ocean.

The grind, as the Pilot whale drive is called, has a recorded history since 1584. On Aug. 8, 2013, 107 Long-finned Pilot whales were slaughtered in Sandavágur, on Vagar Island—a Danish territory. On Aug. 11, 21 Pilot whales were butchered in Leynar; similarly, on Aug. 13, 135 were whaled in Húsavík.

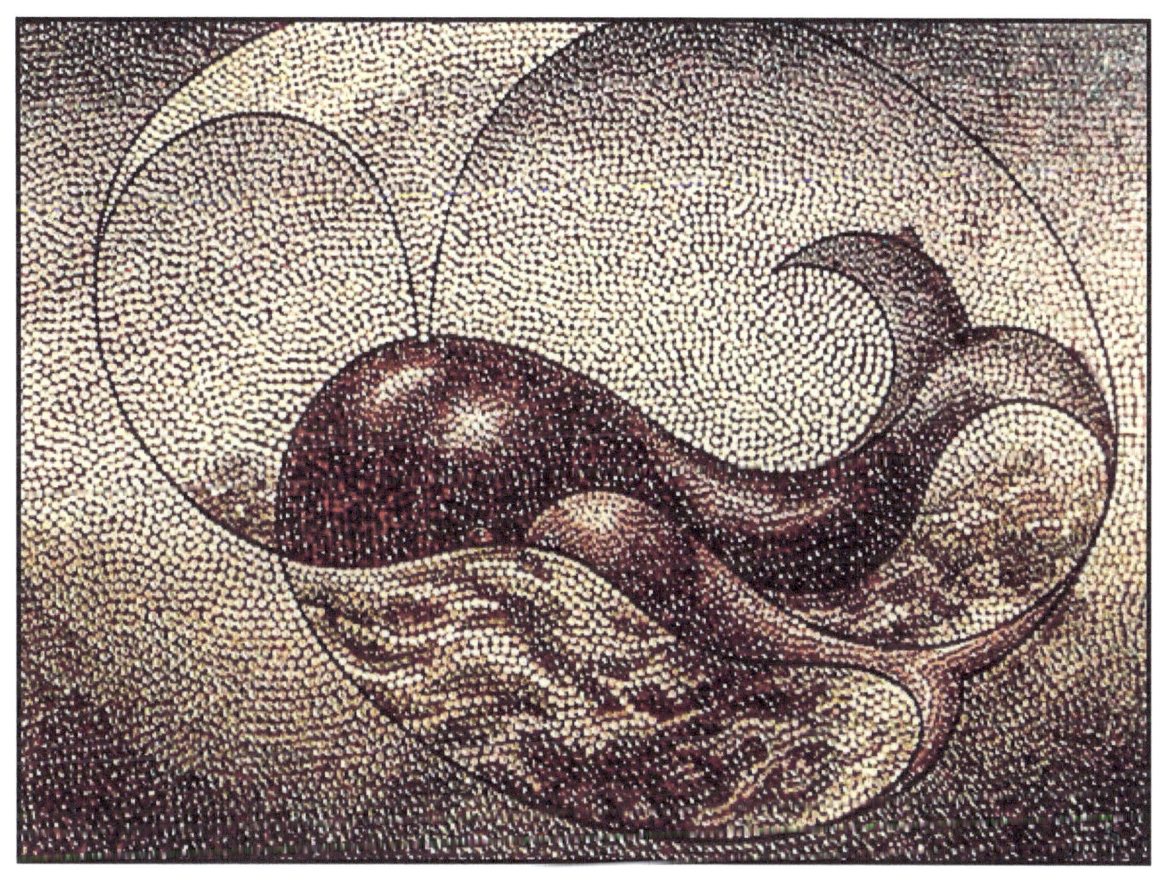

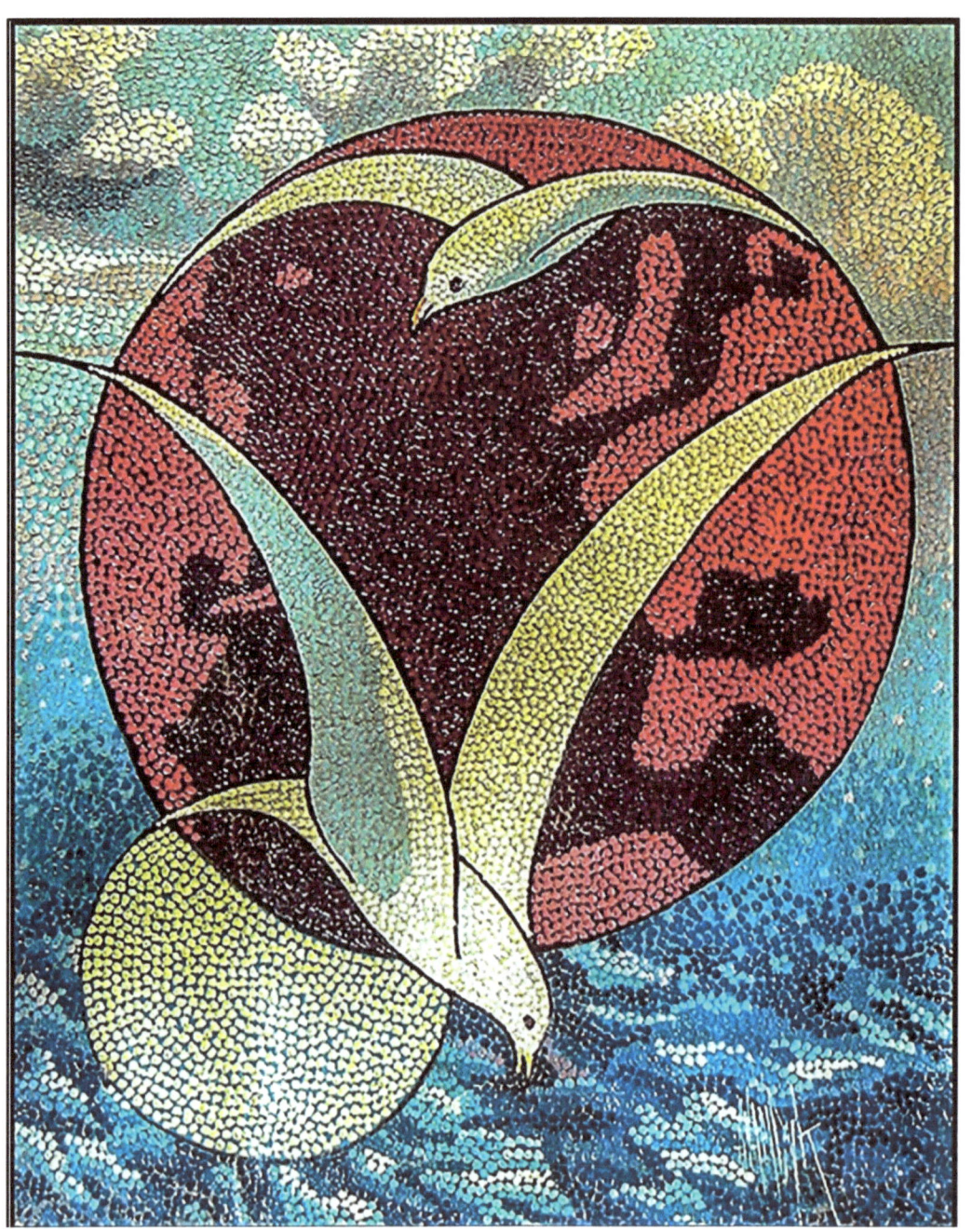

Seagulls Around the World

This piece depicts seagulls and a globe: rendering of seagulls in flight around the world. Seagulls, better known as gulls, have a worldwide cosmopolitan distribution. They breed on every continent, even Antarctica.

In fact, did you know that there are at least 28 types of gull species in North America? Originally, gulls were scavengers of the waters on lakes, rivers or oceans; however, today, they compete with the crows and pigeons in scavenging city parks, backyards, garbage dumps, and food outlets.

Hank's rendition of cosmopolitan distribution is playful and fun with the gulls riding the drafts in the air and floating above the waves.

Two Swans Swimming

Swans are elegantly always in pairs, with a male and female making up the couple. Here, Hank depicts one of such pairs: two swans with their eloquent long necks swimming and feeding peacefully in a lake.

The swan on the left can be observed stopping mid-way to view its reflection as it was about to dip its head in the lake to feed.

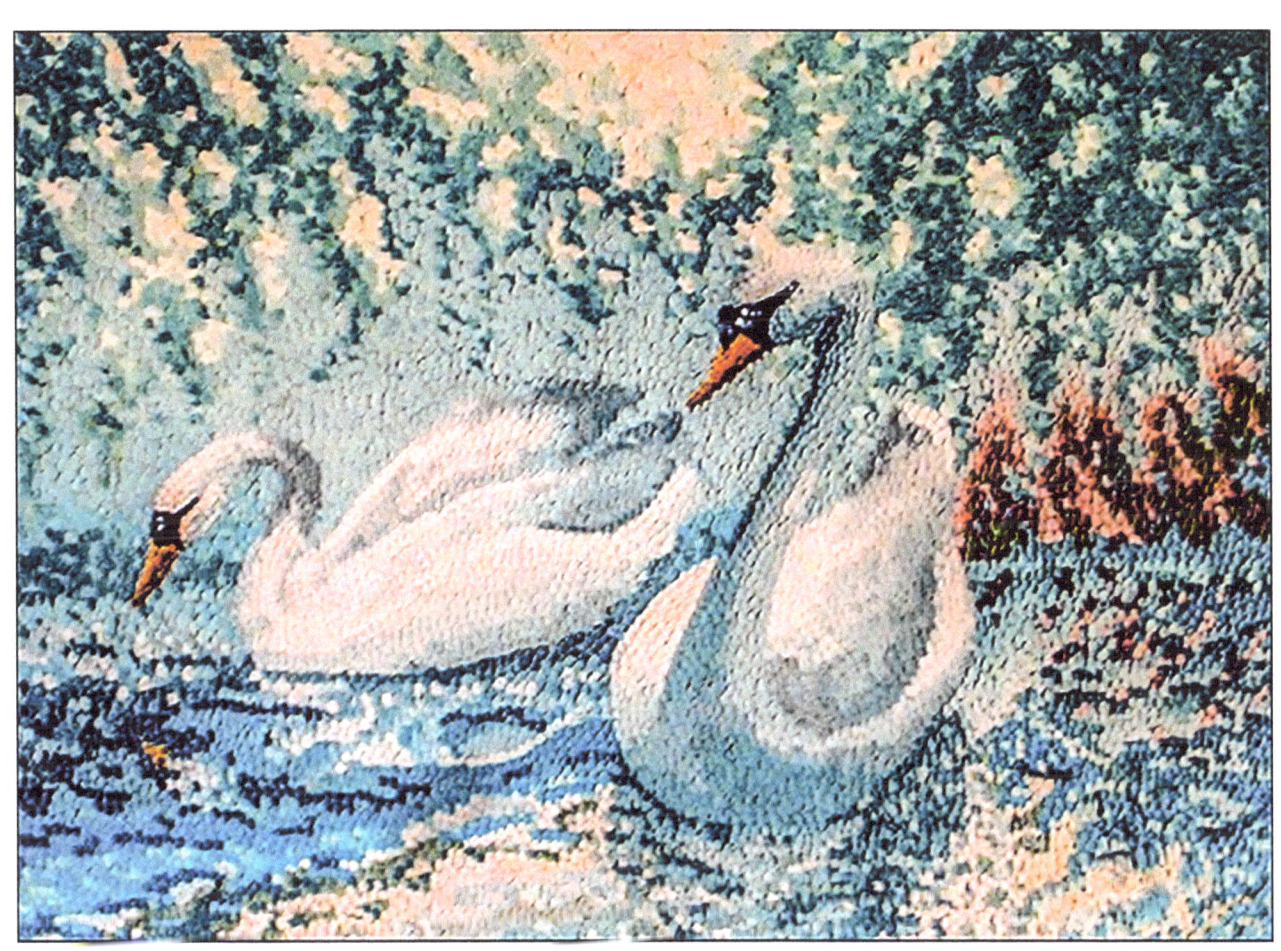

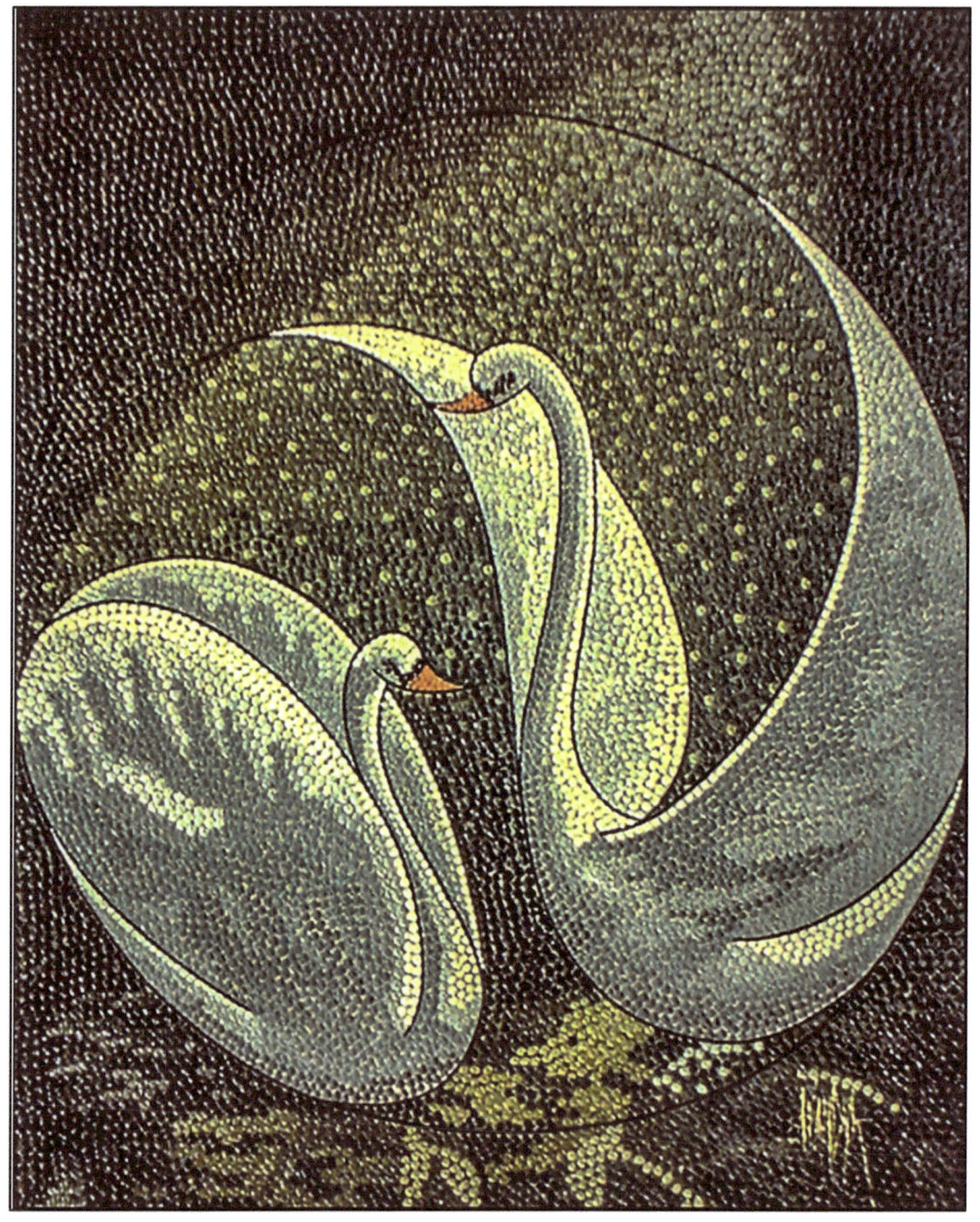

Two Swans

A swan nesting with her partner overlooking. This piece portrays a father swan protecting his family with the utmost care and affection of a loving parent.

Three Flamingos

In this piece, Hank depicts three flamingos wading in the ocean. The first flamingo can be seen feeding, while the one in the middle is squawking, and the last is looking onwards, probably on the lookout for a lurking predator or prey.

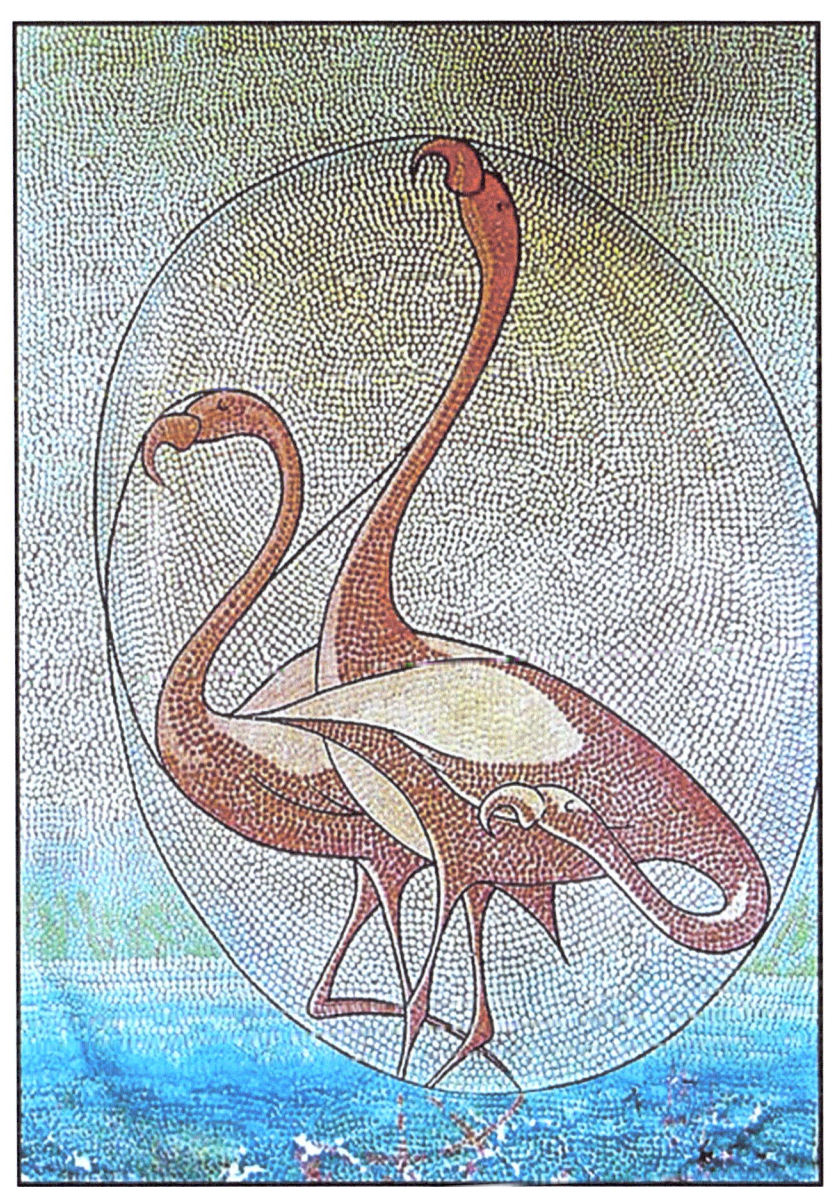

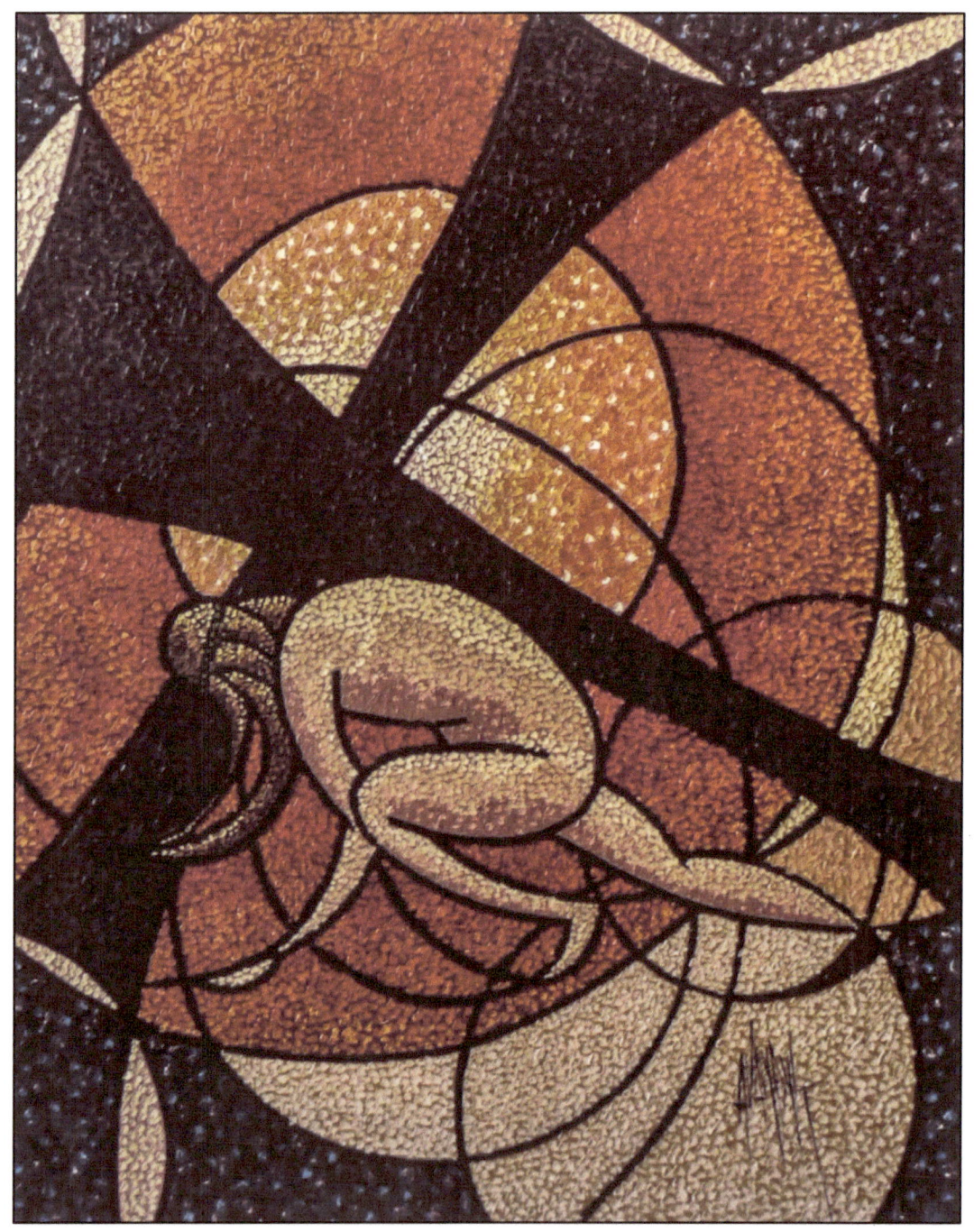

<u>Cross to Bear</u>

This is a depiction of Jesus on the way to His crucifixion. The right foot of Jesus is blackened—a depiction that we all sin.

"We often forget the gravity of our Father's love and His purpose for us on this planet.   We must not forget that blessed is he who calls on the Name of the Lord."

I Am Blue

There was a farmer whose horse ran away. That evening the neighbors gathered to commiserate with him since this was such bad luck. He said, "May be." The next day the horse returned, but brought with it six wild horses, and the neighbors came exclaiming at his good fortune. He said, "May be." And then, the following day, his son tried to saddle and ride one of the wild horses, was thrown, and broke his leg.

Again, the neighbors came to offer their sympathy for the misfortune. He said, "May be." The day after that, conscription officers came to the village to seize young men for the army, but because of the broken leg the farmer's son was rejected. When the neighbors came in to say how fortunately everything had turned out, he said, "May be."

Source: Tao: The Watercourse Way, by Alan Watts

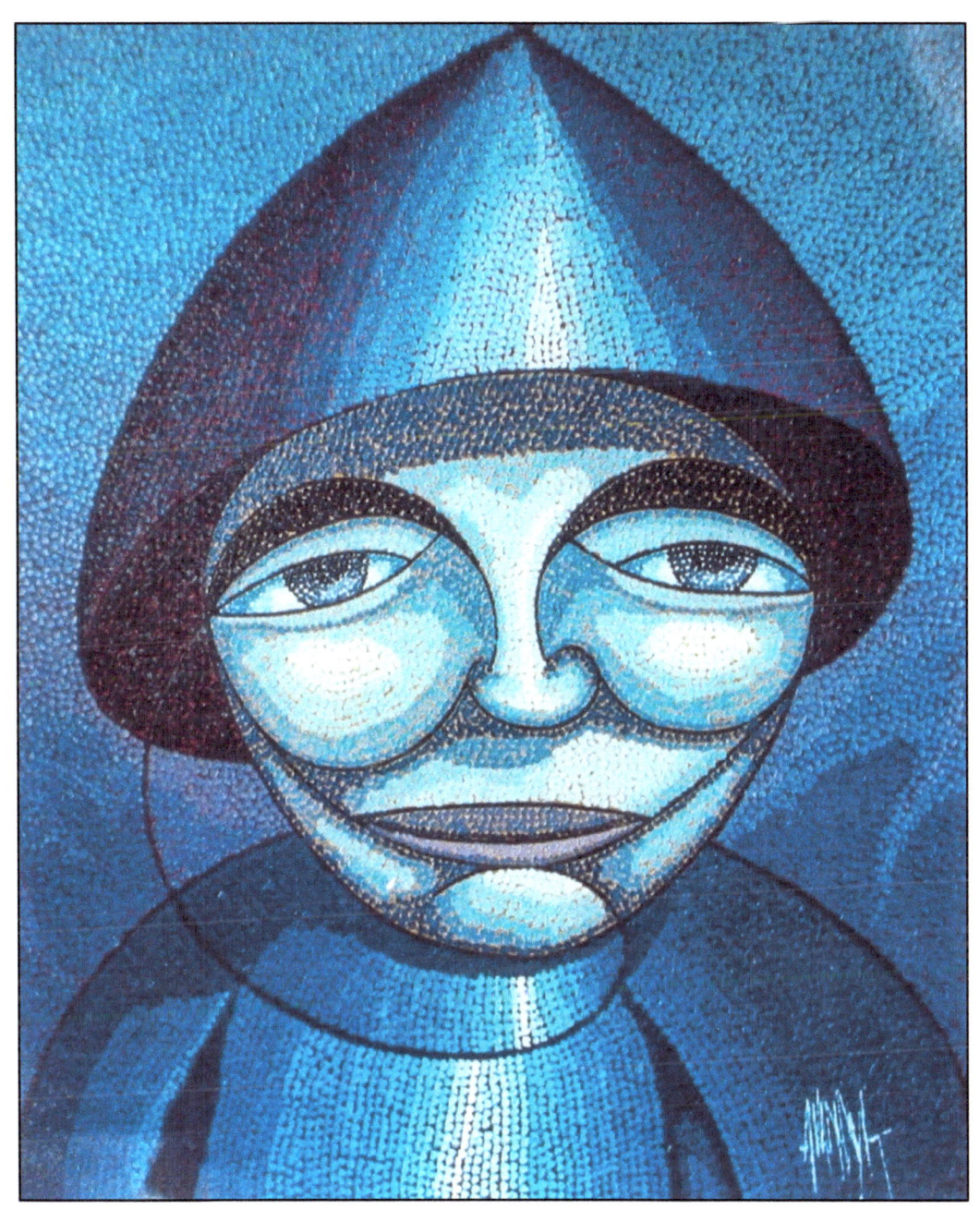

ABOUT THE AUTHOR

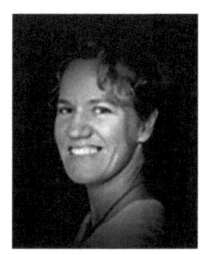

Dorothy Hilde is a mother of two boys. She lives in Saanichton, B.C. She has one grandson, Sawyer, and a mischievous rescue, Dash. She has a passion for photography, gardening, and art. Her favourite past-time is hiking along the seaside or in the dense rain-forest of Vancouver Island with her dog.

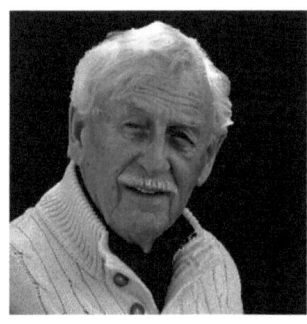

ABOUT THE ARTIST

Hank was born in Sneek, Holland in 1935. He sold his first painting at the age of 14. He enrolled in art school in Amsterdam, where he learned the old Dutch Renaissance style and thereafter became an impressionist.

Hank having somewhat of a gypsy spirit travelled to the United States, Mexico, Western Europe and Spain all the while fine-tuning his technique. He held exhibitions in San Francisco, New Orleans, Mexico City, Valencia, Barcelona, Alicante, Dortmund, Amsterdam, as well as his hometown of Sneek.

It was in the United States that he met Karl Thorp, an impressionistic painter from New York, who was working in New Orleans at the time.

During his stay in Spain, Hank was influenced by Pedro Delso of Barcelona wherein Hank developed his mosaic technique, a technique that is like no other. The paintings truly must be seen in person to experience their true beauty and the emotion Hank has instilled in them.

Shortly thereafter, he met the French artist, Phillipe Dupireux, who was working in the same impressionist manner as another Frenchman, Edzard.

In 1971, the art critic of the Sneeker Newspaper in Holland responded with more than half a page, detailing Hank's life, his work, and his worldwide recognition. In March of 1973, Hank held an exhibition at the art gallery, Sala Rovira, where he received great reviews from the Barcelona Daily News.

Returning to Canada in 1977, Hank returned to his previous realistic style while working exclusively in Vancouver painting landscapes and the coastal scenery of British Columbia.

Hank has since retired from oil painting and has switched over to graphite and pencil crayons to create magical illustrations for children's books. Watch for future collections showcasing Hank's lifetime work! Soon to be published - Landscapes and Seascapes: a collection of graphite, charcoal, pen and ink.

If you would like to purchase prints or originals of Hank's masterpieces go to Fine Art America - Anthony VanDyk.

www.ingramcontent.com/pod-product-compliance
Lightning Source LLC
Chambersburg PA
CBHW051058180526
45172CB00002B/688